Janice Hanna

EVERYDAY

Joy

Spiritual Refreshment for Women

VALUEBOOKS
An Imprint of Barbour Publishing, Inc.

Contents

with emotional problems? Can you truly
"rejoice and be glad" in the midst of such
trials? Of course you can! Joy is a choice,
and it's one the Lord hopes you'll make in
every situation. His joy will give you the
strength you need to make it through.
So, rejoice, dear one. Rejoice!

Anxiety

Know My Heart

Search me, O God,
and know my heart; test me
and know my anxious thoughts.

PSALM 139:23 NLT

Have you ever asked the Lord to give you an "anxiety check"? He longs for you to live in peace, but that won't happen as long as you're driven by worries and fears. Today, allow Him to search your heart. Ask Him to dig deep. Are there cobwebs that need to be swept out? Things hidden that should be revealed? Let God wash away your anxieties, replacing them with His exceeding great joy!

Anxiety. . .
a Joy Killer

Be anxious for nothing, but in
everything by prayer and supplication
with thanksgiving let your requests
be made known to God.

PHILIPPIANS 4:6 NASB

Be anxious for nothing? Is that possible?
Aren't my anxieties tied to my emotions? And
aren't my emotions tied to the things that
happen to me? I can't control what happens
to me, so how can I control my reactions?
Deep breath, friend! Instead of knee-jerking
when troubles come, slip into the throne
room and spend some time giving those
problems to the Lord. With thanksgiving, let
your requests be made known to Him.

An Anxious Heart

A miserable heart means
a miserable life; a cheerful heart
fills the day with song.

PROVERBS 15:15 MSG

Have you ever felt weighted down? Heavy?
Sometimes the cares of this life can make
us so anxious that we only see the tips of our
toes, not the road ahead. Today, lift your
eyes! Speak words of faith and hope over
your situation. Go out of your way to cheer
someone else up. This simple act will lift
your spirits and cause you to forget about
your own burdens. Watch the joy sweep in!

Thou Shalt Not Worry!

"Do not worry about tomorrow,
for tomorrow will worry about itself.
Each day has enough trouble
of its own."

MATTHEW 6:34 NIV

What if the Lord had written an eleventh commandment: "Thou shalt not worry"? In a sense, He did! He commands us in various scriptures not to fret. So, cast your anxieties on the Lord. Give them up! Let them go! Don't let worries zap your strength and your joy. Today is a gift from the Lord. Don't sacrifice it to fears and frustrations! Let them go. . .and watch God work!

Anxious Striving

What does a man get for all the toil
and anxious striving with which
he labors under the sun?

ECCLESIASTES 2:22 NIV

Sometimes, out of anxiety, we bury ourselves in work. We labor from sunup till sundown. There's nothing wrong with working hard, but striving is another thing altogether. When we "strive," we're not trusting God to do His part. We're taking matters into our own hands. Today, take a moment to ask yourself an important question: "Am I working, or am I striving?" Don't let the enemy steal your joy! Strive no more!

Attitude

Attitude Equals Outcome

Serve the LORD with gladness: come before his presence with singing.

PSALM 100:2 KJV

Attitude is everything. Our attitude determines our outcome. We are challenged by scripture to serve with gladness. (It's funny to think of *service* and *gladness* in the same sentence, isn't it?) But here's the truth: If we serve with an attitude of joy, it changes everything. Our service doesn't feel like service anymore. It's a privilege!

Filled with Joy

And the disciples were filled with joy,
and with the Holy Ghost.

ACTS 13:52 KJV

Want to know the secret of walking in
the fullness of joy? Draw near to the Lord.
Allow His Spirit to fill you daily. Let Him
whisper sweet nothings in your ear and
woo you with His love. The Spirit of God is
your Comforter, your Friend. He fills you to
overflowing. Watch the joy flow!

Bubbling Joy

Can both fresh water and salt water flow from the same spring?
JAMES 3:11 NIV

Can you feel it. . .that bubbling in your midsection? Can you sense it rising to the surface? Joy comes from the deepest place inside of us, so deep that we often forget it's there at all. Wonder of wonders! It rises up, up, up to the surface and the most delightful thing happens. Troubles vanish. Sorrows disappear. Godly joy has the power to squelch negative emotions. So, let the bubbling begin!

Joy. . .
Minute by Minute

Keep your eyes focused on what
is right, and look straight
ahead to what is good.

PROVERBS 4:25 NCV

Ever wonder how you can be perfectly
happy one minute and upset the next?
If joy is a choice, then it's one you have to
make. . .continually. We are often ruled by
our emotions, which is why it's so important
to stay focused, especially when you're
having a tough day. Don't let frustration
steal even sixty seconds from you. Instead,
choose joy!

A Word in
Due Season

Everyone enjoys a fitting reply;
it is wonderful to say the right
thing at the right time!

PROVERBS 15:23 NLT

Ever had a friend approach you at just
the right time—say, when you were really
down—and speak something positive and
uplifting? Ah, what perfect timing! You
needed to hear something good, something
pleasant. The right word at the right time
was just what the doctor ordered, causing
joy to spring up in your soul. The next time
you see a friend going through a rough time,
decide to speak that "good word."

Beauty for Ashes

Beauty for Ashes

To appoint unto them that
mourn in Zion, to give unto them
beauty for ashes, the oil of joy
for mourning, the garment of praise
for the spirit of heaviness. . .

ISAIAH 61:3 KJV

Seasons of mourning are difficult to bear, but praise God, He promises to give us beauty for ashes! He pours joy over us like a scented oil. . .to woo us out of periods of grieving. Can you feel it washing down on your head, even now? Can you sense the change in attitude? Slip on that garment of praise, believer! Shake off the ashes! Let God's joy overwhelm you!

The Oil of Joy

Let thy garments be always white;
and let thy head lack no ointment.

ECCLESIASTES 9:8 KJV

What do the words "oil of joy" (Isaiah 61:3) mean to you? Can you envision the Lord anointing you with that precious oil? Do you feel it running over your head and down your cheeks? Oh, that we would always sense the joy of His anointing. That we would see ourselves as usable to the Kingdom. Today, as you enter your prayer time, allow the Lord to saturate you with His oil of joy.

The Garment of Praise

Awake, awake;
put on thy strength, O Zion;
put on thy beautiful garments.

ISAIAH 52:1 KJV

Imagine you've been invited to a grand
celebration—perhaps a wedding or a
banquet. The clothes in your closet are old.
Boring. You need a new outfit, one worthy of
such an occasion. After serious shopping,
you find the perfect dress! It's exquisite and
when you wear it, you're in a party frame of
mind. That's what God desires from each
of us. . .to "dress" ourselves in garments of
praise. It's time to party!

Lifting the Spirit of Heaviness

An anxious heart weighs a man down,
but a kind word cheers him up.

PROVERBS 12:25 NIV

Want to know how to get beyond a season of heaviness? Want to enter a season of joy? Speak uplifting, positive words. The things that come out of your mouth can make or break you. After all, we tend to believe what we hear. So, let words of joy flow. Speak hope. Speak life. And watch that spirit of heaviness take flight!

Shifting Sands

Let us hold unswervingly to the hope we profess, for he who promised is faithful.

HEBREWS 10:23 NIV

Change usually shakes us to the core. However, if you've been in a season of great suffering and you sense change is coming. . .you have reason to celebrate! The sands are shifting. The mourning is coming to an end. God, in His remarkable way, is reaching down with His fingertip and writing, "Look forward to tomorrow!" in the sand. Let the joy of that promise dwell in your heart. . .and bring you peace.

Betrayal

An Offering of Joy

Then my head will be exalted above
the enemies who surround me;
at his tabernacle will I sacrifice
with shouts of joy; I will sing and
make music to the LORD.

PSALM 27:6 NIV

It's one thing to offer a sacrifice of joy when things are going your way and people are treating you fairly. But when you've been through a terrible betrayal, it's often hard to recapture that feeling of joy. As you face hurts and betrayals, remember that God is the Lifter of your head. Sing praises and continue to offer a sacrifice of joy!

A Joyous Defense

But let all who take refuge
in you be glad;
let them ever sing for joy.
Spread your protection over them,
that those who love your name
may rejoice in you.

PSALM 5:11 NIV

Oh, the pain of betrayal. If you've been hurt by someone you trusted, choose to release that person today. Let it go. God is your Defender. He's got your back. Take refuge in Him. And remember, praising Him—even in the storm—will shift your focus back where it belongs. Praise the Lord! He is our defense!

Hang on to
Your Joy!

"The thief comes only to steal and kill and destroy; I have come that they may have life, and have it to the full."

JOHN 10:10 NIV

Have you ever been the victim of a robbery? It's a terrible feeling, isn't it? Who would stoop so low? The enemy of your soul is the ultimate thief. His goal? To steal from you. What is he most interested in? Your peace of mind. Your joy. He often uses betrayal as a mode of operation, so be wary! Next time someone hurts you—or betrays you—don't let him or her steal your joy. Stand firm!

Only Joy Remains

These things have I spoken unto you,
that my joy might remain in you,
and that your joy might be full.

JOHN 15:11 KJV

When you've been badly hurt, it's hard to let go of the pain, isn't it? Sometimes it can crowd out everything—your peace of mind, your enthusiasm, your joy. If you're struggling with the effects of a betrayal today, don't allow it to consume you. Release it to God. Ask Him to replace the pain with His joy—a joy that will remain in you, never to be stolen again.

Come on. . . Get Happy!

But even if you should suffer for
what is right, you are blessed.
"Do not fear what they fear;
do not be frightened."

1 PETER 3:14 NIV

It's one thing to suffer because of something you've done wrong; it's another to suffer for doing right. Even when we're unjustly persecuted, God wants us to respond in the right way. If you're suffering as a result of something you've done for the Lord. . .be happy! Keep a stiff upper lip! This, too, shall pass, and you *can* come through it with a joyful attitude.

Blessing

A Joyous Treasure

"The kingdom of heaven is like treasure hidden in a field. When a man found it, he hid it again, and then in his joy went and sold all he had and bought that field."

MATTHEW 13:44 NIV

Have you ever stumbled across a rare treasure—one so priceless that you would be willing to trade everything you own to have it? If you've given your heart to Christ, if you've accepted His work on Calvary, then you have already obtained the greatest treasure of all. . .new life in Him. Oh, what immeasurable joy comes from knowing He's placed that treasure in your heart for all eternity!

Extraordinary Blessing

There shall be showers of blessing.

EZEKIEL 34:26 KJV

Don't you enjoy walking through seasons of extraordinary blessing? We can hardly believe it when God's "more than enough" provision shines down upon us. What did we do to deserve it? Nothing! During such seasons, we can't forget to thank Him for the many ways He is moving in our lives. Our hearts must overflow with gratitude to a gracious and almighty God.

A Joyful Noise

Make a joyful noise unto the LORD,
all ye lands.

PSALM 100:1 KJV

How do we praise God for His many
blessings? If we follow the pattern of Old
Testament saints, then we lift our voices
in thanksgiving! We let others know. With
a resounding voice, we echo our praises,
giving thanks for all He has done, and all He
continues to do. So, praise Him today! Make
a joyful noise!

Deep Joy

The LORD is my strength and my
shield; my heart trusts in him,
and I am helped. My heart leaps for joy
and I will give thanks to him in song.

PSALM 28:7 NIV

Sometimes our sorrows run deep. We can feel buried alive. That's why it's so important to allow our joys to run deep, too. Today, as you ponder the many things you have to be thankful for, pause a moment. Take a comforting breath. Thank God—from the bottom of your heart—for the deep joys in your life.

Abounding with Blessings

A faithful man shall abound with blessings.

PROVERBS 28:20 KJV

To *abound* means to have more than enough. When you're abounding, all of your needs are met. . .and then some! How wonderful to go through such seasons. So, what do we have to do to qualify for these "more than enough" blessings? Only one thing. Be found faithful. Trust God during the lean seasons. Don't give up! Then, when the "abounding" seasons come, you can truly rejoice!

The Body Of Christ

Joy in Unity

Then make my joy complete by
being like-minded, having the same
love, being one in spirit and purpose.

PHILIPPIANS 2:2 NIV

Want to know how to bring joy to God's
heart? Live in unity with your Christian
brothers and sisters. When we're like-
minded, it pleases our heavenly Father.
Are there problems to be ironed out with a
Christian friend? Troubles in your church
family? Let this be the day you fulfill His
joy by resolving those differences. Let
unity lead the way!

Infectious Joy

How lovely on the mountains are the
feet of him who brings good news,
who announces peace and brings
good news of happiness.

ISAIAH 52:7 NASB

Ever had a contagious illness? Something
like chicken pox or measles? Maybe a bad
cold? Surely you did your best *not* to share
it with your friends and coworkers. Joy is a
lot like that. It's contagious. You can spread
it without even meaning to. Pretty soon all
of your Christian brothers and sisters are
catching it. Now, that's one virus you don't
need to worry about. . .so, spread the joy!

Joyous Members

The body is a unit, though it is made
up of many parts; and though all its
parts are many, they form one body.
So it is with Christ.

1 CORINTHIANS 12:12 NIV

It's fun to look around the church on any
given Sunday morning and see the various
gifts at work. One teaches, the other leads
worship. One edifies, another handles
the finances. God didn't make us all alike.
Praise Him for that! He recognizes our
differences. How do we merge all of those
unique people into one body? We don't!
That's God's job. We simply do our best to
remain unified members of a joyous family.

In the Midst of the Church

Saying, I will declare thy name unto my brethren, in the midst of the church will I sing praise unto thee.

HEBREWS 2:12 KJV

The most amazing thing happens when we gather together in our various churches. When we lift our voices in joyous praise to the Lord, something majestic occurs. In the very midst of our praise, God declares Himself to His people. He's there! The next time you gather together with fellow believers for a time of worship, pause a moment and reflect on the fact that you're entering into God's presence. . .together!

Joy in Serving

So we, being many,
are one body in Christ, and
every one members one of another.

ROMANS 12:5 KJV

There's a lot of work to be done in the local church. Someone has to teach the children, vacuum the floors, prepare meals for the sick, and so forth. With so many needs, how does the body of Christ function without its various members feeling taken advantage of? If you're in a position of service at your local church, praise God for the opportunity to serve others. Step out. . .with joy leading the way.

Changing Seasons

A New Season

> "A woman giving birth to a child
> has pain because her time has come;
> but when her baby is born she forgets
> the anguish because of her joy that
> a child is born into the world."

JOHN 16:21 NIV

If you've ever delivered a child, you know the pain associated with childbirth. But that's not what you remember after the fact, is it? No. As you hold that little one in your arms, only one thing remains. . .the supernatural joy you experience as you gaze into your newborn's eyes. The same is true with the seasons we walk through. Sorrows will end, and joy will rise to the surface once again!

Turn, Turn, Turn

To every thing there is a season,
and a time to every purpose
under the heaven.

ECCLESIASTES 3:1 KJV

Oh, those changing seasons! We watch in
wonder as the vibrant green leaves slowly
morph into dry brown ones, eventually
losing their grip on the trees and drifting
down to the ground below. Change is never
easy, particularly when you have to let go
of the past. But oh, the joy of recognizing
that God sees into the future. He knows
that springtime is coming. Our best days
are ahead!

The Joy Set before Me

> Let us fix our eyes on
> Jesus, the author and perfecter
> of our faith, who for the joy
> set before him endured the cross,
> scorning its shame, and sat down at
> the right hand of the throne of God.

HEBREWS 12:2 NIV

Jesus walked through many seasons in His ministry here on earth. He walked through seasons of great favor, when crowds flocked to Him and when voices cried out, "Blessed is He who comes in the name in the Lord!" But He also walked through seasons of ultimate rejection as He headed up Golgotha's hill. We will go through good times and bad, but, like Jesus, we can say, "But for the joy set before me. . .I will endure."

Change Is
around the Bend

"I will bless them and the places
surrounding my hill. I will send down
showers in season; there will
be showers of blessing."

EZEKIEL 34:26 NIV

How do we shift from one project to the next? One phase of life to the next? We can move forward with joy leading the way when we realize that God is the Giver of the seasons. He designed them and showers us with blessings as we move through each one, even the tough ones! Good news! Change is always just around the bend. Oh, the joy of knowing the hard times won't last.

Good News, Bad News

And they left the tomb quickly with fear and great joy and ran to report it to His disciples.

MATTHEW 28:8 NASB

Ever had a day where all of the news was good? You picked up the phone. . .good news. Read an e-mail. . .good news. Then, the very next day, all of the news was bad! How do we make sense of it all? Even those closest to Jesus went through ups and downs. One moment they mourned His death. . .the next, they celebrated His resurrection. Whether the news is good or bad—choose joy.

40

Corporate Praise

Lift Up Your Voice!

And at midnight Paul and Silas prayed,
and sang praises unto God: and the
prisoners heard them.

ACTS 16:25 KJV

Are you a closet praiser? Happy to worship God in the privacy of your own home but nervous about opening up and praising Him in public? Oh, may this be the day you break through that barrier. Corporate praise—coming together with your brothers and sisters in the Lord to worship Him—is powerful! May you come to know the fullness of His joy as you worship side by side with fellow believers!

A Song of Praise to Him

Let the children of Zion
be joyful in their King.

PSALM 149:2 KJV

Something about the voices of children lifted in joyous praise does something to the heart, doesn't it? Innocent, trusting, filled with pure happiness—their songs ring out for all to hear. Can you imagine how God must feel when we, His children, lift our voices, singing praise to Him? How it must warm His heart! What joy we bring our Daddy God when we praise!

Praise Him in
the Sanctuary

David also ordered the Levite
leaders to appoint a choir of Levites
who were singers and musicians to sing
joyful songs to the accompaniment of
harps, lyres, and cymbals.

1 CHRONICLES 15:16 NLT

It's tough to lift up your voice when you're
feeling down. Sometimes you just don't feel
like praising. However, coming together
as a team—a group—somehow boosts your
strength! Once those instruments begin to
play and the first few words of the songs are
sung, you're suddenly energized as never
before. So, lift your voice with joy in the
sanctuary!

Joy in the Battle

Then they returned, every man
of Judah and Jerusalem,
and Jehoshaphat in the forefront of them,
to go again to Jerusalem with joy;
for the LORD had made them to
rejoice over their enemies.

2 CHRONICLES 20:27 KJV

Enemy forces were just around the bend.
Jehoshaphat, king of Judah, called his
people together. After much prayer, he sent
the worshippers (the Levites) to the front
lines, singing joyful praises as they went.
The battle was won! When you face your next
battle, praise your way through it! Strength
and joy will rise up within you! Prepare
for victory!

Joy. . .a Powerful Force

Praise ye the LORD. Praise God in
his sanctuary: praise him in the
firmament of his power.

PSALM 150:1 KJV

There's just something amazing about
being in a powerful worship service when
all of God's children are like-minded,
lifting up their voices in joyful chorus. The
next time you're in such a service, pause a
moment and listen. . .really listen. Can you
sense the joy that sweeps across the room?
The wonder? Oh, what a powerful force we
are when we praise in one accord!

Disappointment

Rejoicing in the
Hard Times

Yet I will rejoice in the LORD, I will
joy in the God of my salvation.

HABAKKUK 3:18 KJV

Perhaps you've been waiting on pins
and needles for something to happen—
a promised promotion, an amazing
opportunity, something wonderful. Instead,
you get bad news. Things aren't going
to pan out the way you expected. What
do you do now? Instead of giving in to
disappointment, continue to rejoice in the
Lord and watch the disappointment lift. He
will replace your sorrows with great joy.

A Glad Heart

A happy heart makes the face
cheerful, but heartache
crushes the spirit.

PROVERBS 15:13 NIV

Have you ever been so disappointed, so broken-down, that you felt you couldn't go on? Don't despair! Even in the hardest of times, it's possible to have a glad heart. The body reacts to the spirit, so if you want to keep on keepin' on, better do a heart check! No doubt, the cheerful expression on your face is sure to make others ask, "What's her secret?"

Disappointment. . .
Be Gone!

And this hope will not lead
to disappointment.

ROMANS 5:5 NLT

Tired of being disappointed time and time again? Ready for things to change? Try hope. Hope never leads to disappointment. When you're hopeful, you are anticipating good things, not bad. And even if the "good things" you're waiting on don't happen right away, you're energized with joy until they do. So, wave good-bye to disappointment. Choose hope. Choose joy.

Be a God-Pleaser

To the man who pleases him,
God gives wisdom, knowledge
and happiness, but to the sinner he
gives the task of gathering and storing
up wealth to hand it over to the
one who pleases God. This too is
meaningless, a chasing after the wind.

ECCLESIASTES 2:26 NIV

Have you ever watched someone chase after fame, fortune, or wealth? Maybe you've secretly longed for those same things. Instead of chasing after the things this world can offer, which are nothing more than wind, chase after God. Be a God-pleaser. Store up *His* treasures. He is the giver of all things and will make sure you have all you need. . . and more. What joy in finding that treasure!

Rejoice. . .It's Worth Repeating!

Rejoice in the Lord always;
again I will say, rejoice!

PHILIPPIANS 4:4 NASB

Have you ever had to repeat yourself to a child, a spouse, or a coworker? When we want to get our point across—or think someone's not listening as he or she should—we repeat our words. God knows what it's like! Some things are worth repeating, just because they're so good! "Rejoice in the Lord always: and again I say, Rejoice!" He tells us not just once, but twice. Better listen up!

Eternity

Eternal Joy!

And the ransomed of the LORD shall return, and come to Zion with songs and everlasting joy upon their heads: they shall obtain joy and gladness, and sorrow and sighing shall flee away.

ISAIAH 35:10 KJV

Have you ever pondered eternity? Forever and ever and ever. . . ? Our finite minds can't grasp the concept, and yet one thing we understand from scripture: We will enter eternity in a state of everlasting joy and gladness. No more tears! No sorrow! An eternal joy-fest awaits us! Now that's something to celebrate!

Enter into the Joy

His lord said unto him, Well done,
thou good and faithful servant:
thou hast been faithful over a few things,
I will make thee ruler over many things:
enter thou into the joy of thy lord.

MATTHEW 25:21 KJV

When you think of standing before the Lord—face-to-face—are you overwhelmed with fear or awestruck with great joy? Oh, what a glorious day it will be, when we hear Him speak those words, "Well done, thou good and faithful servant." When He ushers us into the joy of His presence for all eternity, our fears and hesitations will be forever washed away. Spend time in joyous rehearsal today!

The Joy of Heaven

I saw the LORD sitting upon
his throne, and all the host of
heaven standing on his right hand
and on his left.

2 CHRONICLES 18:18 KJV

What do you think of when you ponder the word *heaven*? What will it be like to walk on streets of gold, to see our loved ones who have gone before us? How thrilling to know we will one day meet our Lord and Savior face-to-face. He has gone to prepare a place for us—and what a place it will be! The joy of eternity is ours as believers. Praise Him!

Joyous Heirs

That being justified
by his grace, we should be
made heirs according to
the hope of eternal life.

TITUS 3:7 KJV

Have you ever been the recipient of an
inheritance? Ever had a family member pass
away, leaving you money or objects? There
is an inheritance that far exceeds anything
we could ever receive in this world. By
God's grace, we are His heirs! What do we
inherit? Eternal life! If you haven't already
done so, place your trust in Christ today and
experience the joy of becoming His child.
Oh, the joy of a godly inheritance!

The Promise
of Eternal Life

And this is what he promised us—
even eternal life.

1 JOHN 2:25 NIV

Ever had a friend or loved one make a promise, only to break it? What about you? Ever broken a promise? We all fail in this area, don't we? Thankfully, God is not a promise breaker. When He promised you would spend eternity with Him if you accepted the work of His Son on the cross. . .He meant it. Doesn't it bring joy to your heart to know God won't break His promises?

Family

Joy in the Family

Now the God of hope fill you with
all joy and peace in believing,
that ye may abound in hope,
through the power of the Holy Ghost.

ROMANS 15:13 KJV

Living in a family environment isn't
always easy. Siblings bicker. Tempers flare.
People get their feelings hurt. If you want to
experience joy in your family, then ask
the Lord to give you hope, especially when
things are going wrong. Through the power
of the Holy Spirit, you can overcome those
obstacles, but you have to address them
head-on. Today, make a list of problems
you're facing, then ask for God's input.

The Fruit of the Spirit

But the fruit of the Spirit is love, joy, peace, longsuffering, gentleness, goodness, faith.

GALATIANS 5:22 KJV

Want to know how to have the ideal family environment? Want to see parents living in peace with the teens, and vice versa? To obtain a joyous family environment, you've got to have a fruit-bowl mentality. Dealing with anger? Reach inside the bowl for peace. Struggling with impatience? Grab a slice of long-suffering. Having a problem with depression? Reach for joy. Keep that fruit bowl close by! It's going to come in handy!

No Greater Joy

I have no greater joy than
to hear that my children are
walking in the truth.

3 JOHN 1:4 NIV

God rejoices in a strong family. To maintain healthiness, it's important to examine where you all stand—as individuals—in your relationship with the Lord. Sometimes we focus on our own spiritual lives but don't pay much attention to where our children are. Today, ask the Lord to show you what you can do to help your children grow in the Lord. As they grow. . .so will your joy. And so will the Lord's!

Open the Windows!

And there you shall eat before the LORD your God, and you shall rejoice in all to which you have put your hand, you and your households, in which the LORD your God has blessed you.

DEUTERONOMY 12:7 NKJV

Did you grow up in a family where laughter was a key ingredient? Whether you grew up in a joyful home or not, it's surely your desire for the family you now have (or may one day have). God desires that your children walk in joy—and that starts with you. Children are, after all, a reflection of their parents. Today, throw open the windows of your home to the possibility of everlasting joy!

Joyful Children

Let Israel rejoice in him that
made him: let the children of Zion
be joyful in their King.

PSALM 149:2 KJV

Oh, the sound of children's joyful voices.
It's like medicine for the sick. Balm for the
weary soul. God longs for His children to
rejoice in Him, to be joyful. And His desire
for the family is no less. What would be the
point of living in a home where everyone
was sour and bitter? Today, ask the Lord
to give every member of your household
a fresh dose of His abiding joy.

Forgiveness

Joy in Forgiveness

Be kind to each other, tenderhearted, forgiving one another, just as God through Christ has forgiven you.

EPHESIANS 4:32 NLT

Forgiveness is an interesting thing. When you release someone from the sin he or she has committed against you, it's almost like setting a bird free from a cage. You've freed that person up to soar. And, in doing so, you've also freed yourself up. No longer do you have to hold on to the bitterness or anger. Letting go means you can truly move forward with your life. . .in joy!

"Forgive Us Our Debts"

"Forgive us our debts, as we also have forgiven our debtors."

MATTHEW 6:12 NIV

Is it true that God only forgives us to the extent that we forgive others? That's what the scripture teaches! It's so important not to hold a grudge. It hurts you, and it hurts the one you're refusing to forgive. If you've been holding someone in unforgiveness, may today be the day when you let it go. There is incredible joy—both in forgiving and *being* forgiven.

Joyous Freedom

Blessed is he whose transgression
is forgiven, whose sin is covered.

PSALM 32:1 KJV

What if you were locked up in a prison
cell for years on end? You waited for the
day when the jailer would turn that key in
the lock—releasing you once and for all. In
a sense, experiencing God's forgiveness
is like being set free from prison. Can you
fathom the joy? Walking into the sunshine
for the first time in years? Oh, praise
Him for His forgiveness today!

Freedom in Forgiveness

"If you forgive the sins of any,
their sins have been forgiven them;
if you retain the sins of any,
they have been retained."

JOHN 20:23 NASB

Ever known someone who simply refused to forgive? It's one thing to cling to past hurts because you're unable to let go; it's another to do so out of spite. There are no stipulations on forgiveness. We must forgive, regardless of what has been done to us. If you are struggling to release someone who's hurt you, ask the Lord to help you. A miracle of joy will take place as you release your grip.

The Capacity to Forgive

Then Peter came to him and asked,
"Lord, how often should I forgive
someone who sins against me?
Seven times?"
"No, not seven times," Jesus replied,
"but seventy times seven!"
MATTHEW 18:21–22 NLT

It's easy to get fed up with people who consistently hurt you and then ask for forgiveness. We grow weary with their promise that they won't do it again. If someone has repeatedly hurt you, ask the Lord to give you wisdom regarding the relationship, then ask Him to give you the capacity to forgive, even when it seems impossible. Surely joy will rise up in your soul as you watch God at work.

Friendship

Joyous Friendships

The sweet smell of perfume and oils is pleasant, and so is good advice from a friend.

PROVERBS 27:9 NCV

Friendship is a wonderful gift from God. A good friend leaves behind a "pleasant scent." And when you find a friend who offers wise counsel, you are doubly blessed! Today, don't just seek to *find* a friend like that; seek to *be* a friend like that. Leave behind a pleasant aroma to those God has placed in your life.

Dividing Joy

Tell this news with shouts of joy
to the people; spread it
everywhere on earth.

ISAIAH 48:20 NCV

Joy is meant to be shared. (It's hard to keep
to yourself, after all!) Think of it like a tasty
apple pie. You can't eat the whole thing, can
you? No, you need to spread the love, share
the slices. So it is with joy. When you're
going through a particularly joyful season,
pass the plates. Sharing is half the fun!

Show Yourself Friendly

A man that hath friends must shew
himself friendly: and there is a friend
that sticketh closer than a brother.

PROVERBS 18:24 KJV

Ever met someone who just seems to have

the gift of friendship? She's a joy to be

around and is always there when you need

her. Perhaps you're that kind of friend

to others. Friendship is a privilege, and

we're blessed to have brothers and sisters

in Christ. But not all friendships are easy.

Today, ask the Lord to show you how to

"show yourself friendly" in every situation.

Oh, the joy of great relationships!

Greeting One Another in Joy

Speak to one another with psalms, hymns and spiritual songs. Sing and make music in your heart to the Lord.

EPHESIANS 5:19 NIV

Want to try a fun experiment? The next time someone asks you how you're doing, instead of responding, "Okay," why not get more specific? Try "I'm blessed!" or "Having an awesome day!" Encourage yourself in the Lord and He will keep those spirits lifted. And encourage one another with words of blessing, as well.

A Joyous Treasure

"I enjoyed your friendship so much.
Your love to me was wonderful."

2 SAMUEL 1:26 NCV

Imagine finding a trunk in your attic.
You've never noticed it before. It's locked,
but you manage to pry it open. Inside,
to your great amazement, you find gold
and silver coins. Hundreds of them! That
treasure is no more special—no more
amazing—than finding a friend. When you
find a "kindred spirit," you've discovered
a priceless treasure. Oh, the joy of a godly
friendship!

Giving

A Receipt of Joy

"When I smiled at them, they could hardly believe it; their faces lit up, their troubles took wing!"

JOB 29:24 MSG

Some folks are natural joy-givers! They thrive on bringing joy to others in their world. If that's your nature, then you need to know that God wants you to *receive* joy, too. It's a dual process. When you give it, like a boomerang, it comes back to you! So, toss out some joy today. It will surely return, filling your heart and bringing a smile to your face!

Pressed Down, Running Over

Give, and it shall be given unto you;
good measure, pressed down, and
shaken together, and running over,
shall men give into your bosom.

LUKE 6:38 KJV

Give, and it shall be given unto you."
Likely, if you've been walking with the Lord
for any length of time, you've heard this
dozens of times. Do we give so that we can
get? No, we give out of a grateful heart, and
the Lord—in His generosity—meets our
needs. Today, pause and thank Him
for the many gifts He has given you.
Do you feel the joy running over?

Giving Thanks

Let us continually offer the sacrifice
of praise to God, that is, the fruit of
our lips, giving thanks to His name.

HEBREWS 13:15 NKJV

What do you think of when you hear the
word *giving*? Money? Gifts? Offerings?
Time? Talents? Treasures? One of the things
we're called to give. . .is thanks! That's right.
So, pause a moment and thank God for His
many blessings in your life. Feels good to
give, doesn't it?

Giving Your Best

" 'You must present as the LORD's portion the best and holiest part of everything given to you.' "

Christians are called to give of their time, talents, and treasures. Think about the time God has given you. What time can you give back, and how? And what about your talents? Ask the Lord to show you how to use them to advance the kingdom. And your treasures? If you're struggling with giving to your local church, make this the day you release your hold on your finances. Give the Lord your very best.

The Gift of
Giving. . .in Secret

For they gave according to their means, as I can testify, and beyond their means, of their own accord.

2 CORINTHIANS 8:3 ESV

Have you ever felt like giving, just to bless someone? Just to bring joy to a friend's heart? Just to lift a burden? There's something rather exciting about giving in secret, isn't there? And when you reach way down deep—giving out of your own need—it's even more fun. Today, take inventory of the people in your life. Who can you bless. . .in secret?

God's Favor

Seasons of Favor

> May those who delight in my
> vindication shout for joy and
> gladness; may they always say,
> "The LORD be exalted, who
> delights in the well-being
> of his servant."
>
> PSALM 35:27 NIV

Do you ever feel like God's favorite child?
Ever marvel at the fact that He continues to
bestow His extraordinary favor upon you,
even when you don't deserve it? God takes
great pleasure in you and wants to bless you
above all you could ask or think. So, when
you're in a season of favor, praise Him.

Shout for joy and be glad! Tell others
about the great things the Lord
has done.

Joy Comes in the Morning

For his anger lasts only a moment,
but his favor lasts a lifetime!
Weeping may last through the night,
but joy comes with the morning.

PSALM 30:5 NLT

Can you picture a lifetime of blessing?
Hard to imagine, isn't it? We think of
"seasons" of blessing, but God continually
pours out His favor upon His children. We
have our ups and downs—our sorrows and
our joys—but God remains consistent,
never changing. We weep in the bad times
and celebrate during the good. Oh, if only
we could remember that on the tail end of
every sorrow there is a joyful tomorrow!

Joyous Favor

May the favor of the Lord our God
rest upon us; establish the work
of our hands for us—yes,
establish the work of our hands.

PSALM 90:17 NIV

It's interesting to think of "favor" and "the work of our hands" in the same sentence, isn't it? In God's economy, favor equals usefulness. We want the work of our hands to make a difference in this world, and we want to see God smiling down on our ventures. Today, ask God to establish the work of your hands. Then watch as His favor rests upon you!

Finding Favor

**But Noah found favor
in the eyes of the LORD.**

GENESIS 6:8 NIV

Ever wonder why Noah stood out head and
shoulders above others in his generation?
Why did God look upon him with favor?
Noah walked with God and was righteous.
Do you have what it takes to be a "Noah"
in this generation? Walk with God daily.
Don't let the things of this world zap your
strength. Trust Him, live for Him, and
watch Him rain down favor in your life!

Who Exalts?

No one from the east or the west
or from the desert can exalt a man.
But it is God who judges: He brings
one down, he exalts another.

PSALM 75:6–7 NIV

Sometimes we grumble when others are
exalted. We feel left out. Why do others
prosper when everything around us seems
to be falling apart? We can't celebrate
their victories. We aren't joyful for them.
Shame on us! God chooses who to exalt. . .
and when. We can't pretend to know His
thoughts. But we can submit to His will and
celebrate with those who are walking
through seasons of great favor.

God's Love

Amazing Love

He remembered his Covenant with
them, and, immense with love,
took them by the hand.

PSALM 106:45 MSG

You are loved. . .incredibly, sacrificially
loved by the King of kings. Doesn't that fill
you with overwhelming joy? Can you sense
His heart for you? God's love is not based on
anything you have done or will ever do. No.
That amazing love was poured out on Calvary
and beckons us daily. You are loved—today
and always!

"For God So Loved. . ."

For God so loved the world,
that he gave his only
begotten Son, that whosoever
believeth in him should not perish,
but have everlasting life.

JOHN 3:16 KJV

The ultimate expression of love, one that
will never be surpassed, took place when
God sent Jesus, His only Son, to die on the
cross for our sins. "For God so loved. . .that
He gave. . ." That's what love does. It gives
and gives and gives. Love is sacrifice—and
in the person of Jesus Christ we witness the
ultimate sacrifice. Today, as you ponder
God's love for you, rejoice in the fact that
He gave Himself willingly for you.

God Rejoices
over Me

"The LORD your God is with you, he is mighty to save. He will take great delight in you, he will quiet you with his love, he will rejoice over you with singing."

It's fun to picture God celebrating over us, isn't it? Can you imagine? He sings over us! He dances over us. He rejoices over us! What joy floods our souls as we realize our Father God, like a loving daddy, celebrates His love for His children. Today, reflect on the thought that God—with great joy in His voice—is singing over you.

Joyful in Love

Keep yourselves in the love of God,
looking for the mercy of our Lord
Jesus Christ unto eternal life.

JUDE 1:21 KJV

When you love the Lord and recognize
His great love for you, it's easy to be joyful!
Think of His marvelous deeds. Relish in
His overwhelming love for His children.
Recognize His daily blessings. Oh, may we
never forget that the Lord our God longs for
us to see the depth of His love for us. . .and
to love Him fully in return.

Love's Consolation

For we have great joy and
consolation in thy love.

PHILEMON 1:7 KJV

Have you ever found yourself in need of
consolation? Ever longed for someone to
wrap his or her arms of love around you
and make everything all right? God *is* that
Someone. We can take great consolation in
His love, which is unchanging, everlasting,
and abounding. Doesn't it bring joy to your
heart to see how wide, how deep, and how
long the Father's love is for His children?

God's Presence

Joy in His Presence

Splendor and majesty are before him;
strength and joy in his dwelling place.

1 CHRONICLES 16:27 NIV

In Old Testament days, only the high priest could enter the Holy of Holies to spend intimate time with God. However, when Jesus died on the cross, the veil in the temple was torn in two! We now have free access to the Holy of Holies, and Jesus bids us enter. . .often! He longs to spend time with us in that place. And oh, what joy, when we enter in! Make that choice today.

Make a Joyful Noise

Let us come before His presence
with thanksgiving, let us shout
joyfully to Him with psalms.

PSALM 95:2 NASB

Sometimes we forget that the Lord
loves us to praise joyfully. We get caught
up in tradition, or maybe we just feel
uncomfortable worshipping with abandon.
The Lord loves a happy heart—and He truly
enjoys it when we make a joyful noise,
lifting up our praises (our psalms) for all
to hear. So, break out of the box today!
Be set free. . .to worship!

Fullness of Joy

You make known to me the path of life; in your presence there is fullness of joy; at your right hand are pleasures forevermore.

PSALM 16:11 ESV

When we stay on God's path—His road—we experience fullness in every area. And if we stick close to Him, which we are called to do, we will experience joy—not just now, in this life, but forevermore. Can you imagine. . .a joy that never ends? Draw near to the Lord. In His presence you will find fullness of joy.

Joyous Refreshing

"Repent, then, and turn to God,
so that your sins may be wiped out,
that times of refreshing may
come from the Lord."

ACTS 3:19 NIV

Think of a chalkboard, like the one your teacher used in school. What if every bad thing you'd ever done was written on the board? (Shivers!) Now envision the teacher taking the eraser and blotting it all out. Wiping it away. As you watch those sins disappear, you are flooded with joy. Your soul is refreshed. The past no longer holds you back. Give your heart to the Lord, and watch the refreshing come!

Dwelling in Joy

Surely the righteous will praise
your name and the upright will
live before you.

PSALM 140:13 NIV

Have you ever gone camping in a tent?
What if you had a special place—a quiet,
private place like that tent—where you could
dwell with God? A private place of worship?
Wouldn't you want to linger inside that holy
habitat, separating yourself from the outside
world? Pitch your tent today. . .and spend
some time inside with the King of kings.

Health Issues

Joyous Endurance

Behold, we count them happy which
endure. Ye have heard of the patience
of Job. . .that the Lord is very pitiful,
and of tender mercy.

JAMES 5:11 KJV

It's interesting to think of the words *happy*
and *endure* in the same sentence. Twenty-
first-century Christians are accustomed to a
fast-paced life, used to getting what they want
when they want it. But sometimes patience is
required, especially when we're not feeling
well. Want to know the secret of surviving the
seasons that try your patience, the ones that
wear you to a frazzle? Endure! And happiness
will prevail!

A Happy Heart

Therefore my heart is glad and
my glory [my inner self] rejoices;
my body too shall rest and
confidently dwell in safety.

PSALM 16:9 AMP

Ever wish you could take a day off? Feel
like you're always running full-steam
ahead? The Lord designed our bodies to
require rest, and if we skip that part of the
equation, we suffer the consequences! If
you want your body to "confidently dwell
in safety," then you must get the rest you
need. Rest makes for a happy heart. . .and a
healthy body.

A Sacrifice of Praise

Is any among you afflicted?
let him pray. Is any merry?
let him sing psalms.

JAMES 5:13 KJV

It's tough to praise when you're not feeling well, isn't it? But that's exactly what God calls us to do. If you're struggling today, reach way down deep. . . . Out of your pain, your weakness, offer God a sacrifice of praise. Spend serious time in prayer. Lift up a song of joy—even if it's a weak song! You'll be surprised how He energizes you with His great joy!

Be of Good Cheer

A cheerful disposition is good
for your health; gloom and doom
leave you bone-tired.

PROVERBS 17:22 MSG

Want to stay in the best possible health?
Do you take vitamins every day? Eat right?
Exercise? Here's one more thing you can
add to your daily regimen for good health—
a prescription for long life: cheerfulness.
Yes, that's right! To ward off disease, try
joy. According to the proverb above, it's the
very flower of health. And it's just what the
doctor ordered.

The Prayer
of Faith

And the prayer of faith shall save the sick, and the Lord shall raise him up.

JAMES 5:15 KJV

Have you ever wondered why God instructed church leaders to pray for the sick? Perhaps it's because, when we're sick, we often don't have the strength to pray for ourselves. We need our brothers and sisters in the Lord to cry out on our behalf. If you're struggling with illness, call for your Christian friends or church leaders to come and pray with you. What joy. . .when healing comes!

Hope

Joyous Hope

May the God of hope fill you with all joy and peace as you trust in him, so that you may overflow with hope by the power of the Holy Spirit.

ROMANS 15:13 NIV

Isn't it fun to think about God pouring joy into our lives? Imagine yourself with a water pitcher in hand, pouring out, out, out. . .covering everything in sight. The Lord wants us, through the power of the Spirit, to overflow. To bubble over. To experience not just joy, but hope—a benefit of joy. Today, as you spend time in prayer, allow God to saturate you with His joyous hope.

Our Hope, Our Joy

For what is our hope, or joy,
or crown of rejoicing? Is it not even
you in the presence of our Lord
Jesus Christ at His coming?

1 THESSALONIANS 2:19 NKJV

Isn't it funny how the words *hope* and *joy*
just seem to fit together? You rarely find one
without the other. If you have hope in the
unseen tomorrow, then joy rises up in your
soul to give you strength for the journey.
Spend time in God's holy presence today.
In that place, you will find both hope. . .
and joy.

Childlike Hope

For you have been my hope,
O Sovereign LORD, my
confidence since my youth.

PSALM 71:5 NIV

Remember how, as a child, you waited on pins and needles for Christmas to come? You hoped against hope you would get those toys you asked for. You knew in your knower that good things were coming. That same level of expectation can motivate you as an adult. Your Father wants you to trust Him with childlike faith. Put your trust in Him. . .and watch how He moves on your behalf.

Joyous
Perspective

Let us draw near to God with a
sincere heart in full assurance of faith.

HEBREWS 10:22 NIV

Ever looked through a pair of binoculars?
What if you peered through the lenses
and caught a glimpse of God's face? What
if you could see things the way He sees
them? Hear things the way He hears them?
What an amazing perspective! Every time
you draw near to God, He offers you the
opportunity to see Him. To find Him. To
trust Him. Let Him give you His joyous
perspective today.

Unexpected Joy

> Do not be conformed to this world,
> but be transformed by the
> renewing of your mind.
>
> ROMANS 12:2 NKJV

Do you ever find yourself worrying about
tomorrow? Not sure of what it will bring?
Oh, what hope lies in the unseen tomorrow!
What unexpected joys are just around the
corner. Sure, you can't see them. . .but
they're there! Before you give in to fear,
allow the Lord to transform your mind.
See tomorrow as He sees it—filled with
unexpected joys.

Impossible Situations

Joy. . .in Spite of. . .

"Until now you have not asked
for anything in my name.
Ask and you will receive,
and your joy will be complete."

JOHN 16:24 NIV

Have you ever faced a truly impossible situation? One so extreme that, unless God moved, everything else would surely crumble? God is a God of the impossible. And He wants us to ask, even when we're facing insurmountable obstacles. In fact, He wants us to know that only He can perform miracles. Our job? We're called to trust Him. Then, when those impossible situations turn around, our "joy tank" will be completely filled to overflowing!

I *Will* Rejoice!

This is the day the LORD has made;
let us rejoice and be glad in it.

PSALM 118:24 NIV

Are you having a hard day? Facing
mounting problems? Maybe the bill
collectors are calling or the kids are sick.
You're at the end of your rope. Pause for
a moment and remember: *This is the day
which the Lord has brought about. I will
rejoice.* It's His day, and He longs for you
to spend time with Him. Rejoice! It's the
right choice.

Brought Forth
with Joy

And he brought forth his people with joy, and his chosen with gladness.

PSALM 105:43 KJV

Have you ever been delivered out of a terrible situation? Lifted out of it, unharmed? Were you stunned when it happened? Had you given up? God is in the deliverance business! And when He lifts us out of impossible situations, we are overwhelmed with joy. . .and we're surprised! Why do we doubt His goodness? The next time you're in a tough spot, expect to be "brought forth with joy."

The Joy of the Lord
Is Your Strength

"This day is sacred to our Lord.
Do not grieve, for the joy of the
LORD is your strength."

NEHEMIAH 8:10 NIV

Is it possible to have joy in the middle
of catastrophic circumstances? What if
you're facing the loss of a job? A devastating
illness? The death of a loved one? Can you
really look beyond your grief to find the joy?
Our very strength comes from the joy God
places inside us, and we need that strength
even more when we're facing seemingly
impossible odds! Today, may God's joy
strengthen you from the inside out.

Exceeding Joy

But rejoice, inasmuch as ye are partakers of Christ's sufferings; that, when his glory shall be revealed, ye may be glad also with exceeding joy.

1 PETER 4:13 KJV

We want to know Christ—both in the glory of His resurrection and in the fellowship of His sufferings. If we're open to really knowing Him in both ways, then we've got to be vulnerable. Finding a balance is key. It really is possible to go through times of suffering and still maintain your joy. After all, joy is a choice.

Individual Praise

Make a Joyful Noise

O come, let us sing unto the LORD:
let us make a joyful noise to
the rock of our salvation.

PSALM 95:1 KJV

Do you love to sing praises to God?
Perhaps your voice isn't the best. Maybe
you can't carry a tune in a bucket, but you
long to praise God anyway. Go ahead and do
it! We're told in scripture to "make a joyful
noise" to the Lord. We're not told it has to
be with a trained voice. So, lift up those
praises! He accepts them, on key or off!

A Chorus of Praise

Sing for joy to God our strength;
shout aloud to the God of Jacob!

PSALM 81:1 NIV

Imagine you're in a room filled with noisy,
fussy, crying children. The combination
of their voices raised in miserable chorus
is overwhelming. Now imagine that same
group of children, singing praise to God in
unison. They're making a joyful noise—and
what a pleasant sound it is! Today, as you
face life's many challenges, focus on being
a praise-giver, not a fussy child.

Joyful in Glory

Let the saints be joyful in glory:
let them sing aloud upon their beds.

PSALM 149:5 KJV

When do you like to spend time alone with the Lord? In the morning, as the stillness of the day sweeps over you? At night, when you rest your head upon the pillow? Start your conversation with praise. Let your favorite worship song or hymn pour forth! Tell Him how blessed you are to be His child. This private praise time will strengthen you and will fill your heart with joy!

With Thanksgiving

I will praise the name of God
with a song, and will magnify
him with thanksgiving.

PSALM 69:30 KJV

It's one thing to spend time with God;
it's another to praise Him with a thankful
heart. Sometimes we forget His many
blessings. We praise out of routine. Today,
allow God to remind you of all the many
ways He has blessed you. Oh, what full and
thankful hearts we have when we pause to
remember. Now, watch your praises rise
to the surface, like cream to the top of
the pitcher.

A Big Song

Shout for joy to the LORD,
all the earth, burst into
jubilant song with music.

PSALM 98:4 NIV

Do you ever feel like you don't have enough
words to praise God? Like your vocabulary
is limited? Wish you could throw the lid
off and worship Him with abandon? That's
exactly what He longs to do—spend intimate
time with you. Sing a big song to the Lord.
And prepare yourself for the inevitable joy
that will rise up as you do.

The Journey

The Joyful Sound

Blessed is the people that know the joyful sound: they shall walk, O LORD, in the light of thy countenance.

PSALM 89:15 KJV

Imagine a dimly lit room. You can barely make out the shapes of things around you. Somewhere in that room, your Father is waiting for you. Suddenly His voice rings out and joyous relief floods your soul. Even though you cannot see where you are going, the sound of His voice guides you directly into His arms. Allow yourself to tune in to that precious voice today.

Satisfied by Joy

Satisfy us in the morning with your
unfailing love, that we may sing
for joy and be glad all our days.

PSALM 90:14 NIV

You've heard the adage, "You're only as
old as you feel." One thing that ages us too
quickly is discouragement. We get down,
and it's hard to get back up again. We need
to make a conscious effort each morning to
reach out to God. . .to ask Him to satisfy
us with His mercy, His loving-kindness.
If we're truly satisfied, joy will come. And
joy is the best antiwrinkle cream on the
market.

Joy in the Journey

I press toward the mark for the prize of the high calling of God in Christ Jesus.

Ever feel like the journey's too long? Like you're not making progress? Today, ask the Lord to give you joy as you make your way toward the goal. Don't fret if things aren't happening as quickly as you want them to. Keep on pressing toward the mark. Thank Him for the process, and take time to truly take "joy in the journey."

Finishing with Joy

But none of these things move me,
neither count I my life dear unto
myself, so that I might finish
my course with joy.

ACTS 20:24 KJV

The Christian life is a journey, isn't it?
We move from point *A* to point *B*, and then
on from there—all the while growing in
our faith. Instead of focusing on the ups
and downs of the journey, we should be
looking ahead to the finish line. We want to
be people who finish well. Today, set your
sights on that unseen line that lies ahead.
What joy will come when you cross it!

The Joy of
His Heart

For he shall not much remember
the days of his life; because God
answereth him in the joy of his heart.

ECCLESIASTES 5:20 KJV

Sometimes we go through things that we wish we could forget. Hard things. Hurtful things. But God, in His remarkable way, eases the pain of our bumps in the road and before long, we can barely remember them. Joy rises up in place of pain, and we move forward, content in the fact that tomorrow will be better than yesterday. Don't focus on yesterday. Live for today and look forward to tomorrow.

Living the Life

Righteousness, Peace, and Joy

For the kingdom of God is not meat and drink; but righteousness, and peace, and joy in the Holy Ghost.

ROMANS 14:17 KJV

Sometimes life can be drudgery. We wake up in the morning. Get dressed. Go to work (or stay home to care for our children). We drag home in the evening, spend a little time with our loved ones, then drop into bed, exhausted. Oh, there's so much more to life! The Lord wants to remind you that He has given you righteousness, peace, and joy. . .for every day of your life! So, celebrate!

Everyday Joy

For in him we live, and move, and have our being.

ACTS 17:28 KJV

Every breath we breathe comes from God. Every step we take is a gift from our Creator. We can do nothing apart from Him. In the same sense, every joy, every sorrow. . .God goes through each one with us. His heart is for us. We can experience joy in our everyday lives, even when things aren't going our way. We simply have to remember that He is in control. We have our being. . .in Him!

A Life of Joy

You have greatly encouraged me
and made me happy despite
all our troubles.

2 CORINTHIANS 7:4 NLT

Want to know the perfect recipe for happiness? Spend your days focused on making others happy. If you shift your focus from yourself to others, you accomplish two things: You put others first, and you're always looking for ways to make others smile. There's something about spreading joy that satisfies the soul.

The Ways of Life

" 'You have made known to me
the paths of life; you will fill me
with joy in your presence.' "

ACTS 2:28 NIV

God gives us everything we need to make
it through life. He teaches us His ways.
Fills us with His joy. Gives us the pleasure
of meeting with Him for times of intimate
worship. What an awesome teacher and
friend. He takes us by the hand and gently
leads us. . .from experience to experience. . .
joy to joy.

Christ Lives in Me

I am crucified with Christ:
nevertheless I live; yet not I,
but Christ liveth in me.

GALATIANS 2:20 KJV

When you gave your heart to Christ, the old you—the person you used to be—died. She's no longer alive. In a symbolic sense, you rose up out of that experience with God as a new creature—never again the same. So, the life you now live isn't really your own. It's His! And He lives in you. What a joyful exchange!

Mercy

Blessings on the Merciful

"Blessed are the merciful,
for they shall obtain mercy."

MATTHEW 5:7 NKJV

In some ways, mercy is like forgiveness.
God offers it to the same extent we're willing
to give it to others. The more merciful we
are toward those who wrong us, the more
merciful God is to us. And blessings flow
out of relationships that extend mercy. Want
to experience true joy today? Give. . .and
receive. . .mercy.

His Mercy
Endures Forever

O give thanks unto the LORD;
for he is good: for his mercy
endureth for ever.

PSALM 136:1 KJV

God's mercy endures forever. It never
ends. What about *our* mercy? How long
does it endure? Until our patience is tested?
Until someone rubs us the wrong way?
Until we're hurt or offended by a friend or
coworker? If God's mercy endures forever,
we should strive to be merciful, too. After
all, if the King of kings offers it repetitively,
shouldn't we do so, as well? Today, extend
mercy. . .and watch the joy flow!

Merciful Joy

It is a sin to hate your neighbor,
but being kind to the needy
brings happiness.

PROVERBS 14:21 NCV

Our loving heavenly Father is so merciful toward us, and He expects us to treat others with mercy, too. Did you realize that having mercy on those who are less fortunate than you can actually make you happy? It's true! Reach out to someone today—and watch the joy start to flow!

Mercy Multiplied

Mercy unto you, and peace,
and love, be multiplied.

JUDE 1:2 KJV

Have you ever done the math on God's
mercy? If so, you've probably figured out that
it just keeps multiplying itself out, over and
over again. We mess up; He extends mercy.
We mess up again; He pours out mercy once
again. In the same way, peace, love, and joy
are multiplied back to us. Praise the Lord!
God's mathematics work in our favor.

Fresh Mercy

The faithful love of the LORD
never ends! His mercies never cease.
Great is his faithfulness; his mercies
begin afresh each morning.

LAMENTATIONS 3:22–23 NLT

Don't you love the newness of morning?
The dew on the grass? The awakening of
the sun? The quiet stillness of the day when
you can spend time alone with the Lord in
solitude? Oh, what joy rises in our souls as
we realize that God's love and mercy are
new every morning! Each day is a fresh
start, a new chance. Grace washes over us
afresh, like the morning dew. Great is His
faithfulness!

The Nations

Joy on That Glorious Day

Yea, all kings shall fall down before
him: all nations shall serve him.

PSALM 72:11 KJV

There's coming a day when every knee will
bow and every tongue confess that Jesus
Christ is Lord. Does it seem impossible
right now, in light of current world events?
If only we could see things the way God
does! He knows that the kings of the nations
will one day fall down before Him. Oh, what
a glorious and joyful day that will be!

Joy for the Nations

Therefore the redeemed of the LORD shall return, and come with singing unto Zion; and everlasting joy shall be upon their head: they shall obtain gladness and joy; and sorrow and mourning shall flee away.

ISAIAH 51:11 KJV

God longs for people across the globe to turn their hearts to Him. He wants them to understand that He sent His only begotten Son to earth to die on a rugged cross so that people of every race, creed, and color could be set free from their sins. Oh, that people around the world would turn to God, would return to Him with singing, and with everlasting joy upon their heads!

Joy in the Cities

And there was great joy in that city.
ACTS 8:8 KJV

Can you imagine the church of Jesus Christ—alive and vibrant in *every* city around the world? Alive in Moscow. Alive in Paris. Alive in Havana. Alive. . .in your hometown. Oh, the celebration that will ensue when cities around the world are eternally changed. Today, choose a particular city and commit to pray for that place. . .that all might come to know Him!

Rejoicing Rulers

The king shall joy in thy strength,
O Lord; and in thy salvation how
greatly shall he rejoice!

PSALM 21:1 KJV

It's so important to pray for our rulers.
They need our undergirding, our daily
intercession, and our prayers for their safety
and wisdom. Today, as you contemplate your
current political leaders, pause a minute
and lift their names up in prayer. May they
all find strength in the joy of the Lord.
May each come to the fullness of salvation.
And may the people rejoice as a result of
what the Lord has done!

Praise Him, All You Nations!

All of you nations, come praise the LORD! Let everyone praise him.

PSALM 117:1 CEV

Can you imagine the sound of millions of people, singing praises to the Lord in thousands of different languages simultaneously? On any given day, God hears people all over the world lift up their praises to Him in their native tongues. Oh, what a joyful sound that must be to our heavenly Father. Today, as you lift your voice, think of the millions of others who join you. Praise Him! Oh, praise Him!

Nature

Nature's Joyous Song

**Let the floods clap their hands:
let the hills be joyful together.**

PSALM 98:8 KJV

All of nature sings the praises of our
mighty God. Look around you! Do you
see the hills off in the distance, pointing
up in majesty? Can you hear the water in
the brooks, tumbling along in a chorus of
praise? And what about the ocean waves?
Oh, the joy in discovering the God of the
universe through His marvelous creation!

Go Out with Joy

For ye shall go out with joy, and be led forth with peace: the mountains and the hills shall break forth before you into singing, and all the trees of the field shall clap their hands.

ISAIAH 55:12 KJV

God reveals Himself in a million different ways, but perhaps the most breathtaking is through nature. The next time you're in a mountainous spot, pause and listen. Can you hear the sound of God's eternal song? Does joy radiate through your being? Aren't you filled with wonder and with peace? The Lord has, through the beauty of nature, given us a rare and glorious gift.

Sing, O Heavens!

Sing, O heavens; and be joyful,
O earth; and break forth into singing,
O mountains: for the LORD hath
comforted his people, and will have
mercy upon his afflicted.

ISAIAH 49:13 KJV

Imagine you're walking through a meadow on a dewy morning. The sweet smell of dawn lingers in the air. Suddenly, like a skilled orchestra, the heavens above begin to pour out an unexpected song of joy. You close your eyes, overwhelmed by the majesty of the moment. Scripture tells us the heavens and the earth are joyful. . . so tune in to their chorus today.

A Joy Forever

The Mighty One, God, the LORD,
speaks and summons the earth
from the rising of the sun to the
place where it sets. From Zion,
perfect in beauty, God shines forth.

PSALM 50:1–2 NIV

A child's face. A flowering pear tree.

A rippling brook. A mountain's peak.

All of these things overwhelm us with the

magnitude of their beauty. Why? Because we

can see that they were created by Someone

much larger than ourselves—Someone

incredibly creative and colorful. We are

reminded of the awesomeness of God. Focus

on the beauty He has placed in your world. . .

and praise Him!

Nature's Joys

The heavens declare the glory
of God; the skies proclaim the
work of his hands.

PSALM 19:1 NIV

Oh, the wonder of God's creation! Who could paint the skies such a brilliant blue? And who could give such detail to such a tiny blade of grass? Only our creative Lord! Spend some time outdoors with Him today, soaking in the beauty of your surroundings. Allow the joy to permeate your soul, and give thanks to our awesome God, Creator of all.

New Beginnings

Second Chances

For his anger lasts only a moment,
but his favor lasts a lifetime; weeping
may remain for a night, but rejoicing
comes in the morning.

PSALM 30:5 NIV

Don't you love second chances? New
beginnings? If only we could go back and
redo some of our past mistakes. . .what
better choices we'd make the second time
around. Life in Jesus is all about the rebirth
experience—the opportunity to start over.
Each day is a new day, in fact. And praise
God! The sorrows and trials of yesterday
are behind us. With each new morning,
joy dawns!

Exceeding Great Joy

When they saw the star, they rejoiced with exceeding great joy.

MATTHEW 2:10 KJV

Can you imagine the wise men, gazing upon that star for the first time? Finally! The long-awaited day had come. What joy they must have felt in their hearts. Surely they could sense the beginning of a new era. The gospel message is all about new beginnings. We rejoice every time we're given a chance to begin again. Praise God for the many times He's given you a fresh start.

Out of the Pit

I waited patiently for the LORD.
He turned to me
and heard my cry.
He lifted me out of the pit of
destruction, out of the sticky mud.
He stood me on a rock and
made my feet steady.

PSALM 40:1–2 NCV

When you've been living in the pit, you can hardly imagine being lifted out of it. Oh, the joy of knowing God can bring us out of even the deepest, darkest pit and place our feet on solid ground. Nothing is impossible with our Lord! If you're in a dark place today, call out to Him. . .and watch as He delivers you. He will establish your steps. Praise Him!

On Wings of Joy

"All the earlier troubles, chaos,
and pain are things of the past,
to be forgotten. Look ahead with joy.
Anticipate what I'm creating."

ISAIAH 65:17–18 MSG

We don't always get it right, do we? Sometimes we make mistakes. But our mistakes spur us on to begin again. We want to get it right the next time. And praise God! He gives us chance after chance, opportunity after opportunity. Let the joys of your past successes merge with the "spurs" of your past failings so that you can set out on a road of new beginnings.

The New Man

And have put on the new self,
which is being renewed in knowledge
in the image of its Creator. . .

COLOSSIANS 3:10 NIV

Are there people in your life you've given up on? Maybe someone you've been praying for, for years? You're convinced he or she will never come to the Lord? Today, ponder the new beginnings in your own life. Hasn't God recreated you? Renewed you? Won't He do the same for others? Feel the joy rise up as you ponder the possibilities? Pray for that friend or loved one to "put on the new self."

Obedience

Joyful Obedience

Now unto him that is able to keep you from falling, and to present you faultless before the presence of his glory with exceeding joy. . .

JUDE 1:24 KJV

Our obedience makes God happy—and should make us happy, too. In fact, the more difficult it is to obey, the more joyful we should be. Why? Because a big situation calls for a big God. And our God is bigger than anything we could ask or think. He alone can prevent us from falling. So, if you're struggling in the area of obedience, surrender your will. Enter into joyful obedience.

Used for a Purpose

Become the kind of container
God can use to present any
and every kind of gift to his
guests for their blessing.

2 TIMOTHY 2:21 MSG

Want to reach the end of your life feeling

completely fulfilled? Want to know true joy?

Then allow the Lord to use you. Does that

idea contradict what you've been taught in

this "me first" society? Being "used" by God

is far different from being "used" by people.

Being usable is our goal, our ambition.

Today, offer your gifts and abilities to

the Lord so that they can be used for His

purpose and His glory.

Something to Talk About

Everyone has heard about your obedience, so I am full of joy over you; but I want you to be wise about what is good, and innocent about what is evil.

ROMANS 16:19 NIV

Ever been caught in a situation where people were talking about you behind your back? Maybe folks you loved and trusted? How did that make you feel? Well, how would you feel if you found out people were talking about you. . .because of your obedience? Wow! That's a different thing altogether. Let them talk! May our joyful obedience to the Lord win us a spot in many cheerful conversations!

Years of Pleasure

If they obey and serve him,
they shall spend their days
in prosperity, and their
years in pleasures.

JOB 36:11 KJV

If you knew that your disobedience was going to cost you dearly, would you be more inclined to obey? If you knew that your obedience would be rewarded, would that spur you on to do the right thing? Scripture convinces us that our days can be spent in prosperity and our years in pleasures if we will simply obey and serve the Lord. Oh, the joy of obedience!

Uprightness

"I know also, my God,
that You test the heart and
have pleasure in uprightness."

1 CHRONICLES 29:17 NKJV

Everyone wants to be happy, right? We
know that our obedience to the Lord results
in a life of great joy. But our obedience does
something else, too. It brings pleasure to
our heavenly Father. When we live uprightly,
God is pleased. Today, instead of focusing
on your own happiness, give some thought
to putting a smile on *His* face.

Overflowing Joy

Limitless Joy

> "I have told you this so that
> my joy may be in you and that
> your joy may be complete."
>
> JOHN 15:11 NIV

Did you realize that joy is limitless?
It knows no boundaries. Jesus poured
Himself out on the cross at Calvary—giving
everything—so that you could experience
fullness of joy. Even now, God longs to
make Himself known to you in such a new
and unique way. May you burst at the seams
with this limitless joy as you enter His
presence today.

Spilling Over

And these things write we unto you,
that your joy may be full.

1 JOHN 1:4 KJV

Imagine you're in the process of filling a glass with water and accidentally pour too much in. The excess goes running down the sides, splashing your hand and anything else it comes in contact with. That's how it is when you're overflowing with joy from the inside out. You can't help but spill out onto others, and before long, they're touched, too. So, let it flow!

I've Got the Joy!

I will greatly rejoice in the LORD,
my soul shall be joyful in my God.

ISAIAH 61:10 KJV

As children we used to sing, "I've got the joy, joy, joy, joy down in my heart!" We bounced up and down in our seats with great glee. Do you still have that joy? Has it lingered into your adulthood? Do you sense it to the point where you could come bounding from your chair, ready to share what He's given you with a lost and dying world? Oh, for such a childlike joy!

Shout for Joy!

Be glad in the LORD and rejoice,
you righteous ones; and shout for joy,
all you who are upright in heart.

PSALM 32:11 NASB

Have you ever been so happy that you just felt like shouting? Ever been so overcome with joy that you wanted to holler your praise from the rooftops for all to hear? Well, what's holding you back? Go for it! Shout for joy! Let the whole world hear your praises to the King of kings!

Joy-Scatterers

Light-seeds are planted in the souls of God's people, joy-seeds are planted in good heart-soil.

PSALM 97:11 MSG

Imagine a farmer dropping seeds into fertile soil. They're sure to spring up. That's how it is with joy. Keep it with you at all times, like seeds in your pocket. Then, when you find fertile soil—in the workplace, at the doctor's office, around the dinner table— pull out a few of those seeds and sprinkle them around. Oh, the joy that will spring forth!

Patience

Joyful Patience

Strengthened with all might,
according to his glorious power,
unto all patience and longsuffering
with joyfulness. . .

COLOSSIANS 1:11 KJV

You've heard the old adage, "Don't pray for patience! God will surely give you a reason to need it!" Here's the truth: As you wait on the Lord, He promises to strengthen you with all might, according to His glorious power. So, what's a little waiting, as long as God is giving you strength? And you know where that strength comes from after all. . . the joy of the Lord *is* your strength!

Wanting Nothing

But let patience have its perfect work, that you may be perfect and complete, lacking nothing.

JAMES 1:4 NKJV

Let patience have its perfect work? Ouch! It's hard enough to wait, even harder to wait patiently. Now we're supposed to let patience "work" in us while we're waiting? Sounds painful. . .and nearly impossible! But when we allow patience to have its perfect work in us, we are "complete," wanting nothing. We can wait patiently. . .and not stress about the yet-unanswered prayers. Every need is met in Him. Talk about joy!

Rejoicing in Hope

[Be] rejoicing in hope;
patient in tribulation;
continuing instant in prayer.

ROMANS 12:12 KJV

The words *rejoice* and *hope* just seem to go together, don't they? There's something about choosing joy that fills our hearts with hope for better days ahead. So what, if we have to wait awhile? If we stay focused on the Lord, casting our cares on Him, that day of rejoicing will surely come!

The Path of Joy

Moses spoke to the people:
"Don't be afraid.
Stand firm and watch GOD do his
work of salvation for you today."
EXODUS 14:13 MSG

When we're waiting on a miracle, the minutes seem to drag by. We force our attentions ahead to tomorrow. . .in the hopes that we'll receive the answer we long for. But what about today? This is the day the Lord has made! He wants us to rejoice in it. So what if the answer hasn't come yet? So what if patience is required? Don't miss the opportunity to connect with God. . .today!

Joyous Tomorrow

But if we hope for that we see not,
then do we with patience wait for it.

ROMANS 8:25 KJV

Are you in a "waiting" season? Is your patience being tested to the breaking point? Take heart! You are not alone. Every godly man and woman from biblical times till now went through seasons of waiting on the Lord. Their secret? They hoped for what they could not see. (They never lost their hope!) And they waited patiently. So, as you're waiting, reflect on the biblical giants and realize. . .you're not alone!

Prayer

Answered Prayers

But the angel said to him,
"Do not be afraid, Zacharias,
for your prayer is heard; and your wife
Elizabeth will bear you a son,
and you shall call his name John."

LUKE 1:13 NKJV

Zacharias, though quite old, had been praying for a child for years. How funny that the angel prepared him by saying, "Don't be afraid," before sharing the news! This answered prayer, though joyous, surely rocked Zacharias and Elizabeth's world! Have you ever consistently prayed for something without getting the answer you want? Ever felt like giving up? Don't! When you least expect it, your answer could come. . .and it just might rock your world!

Approaching the Throne with Joy

In every prayer of mine I always make my entreaty and petition for you all with joy (delight).

PHILIPPIANS 1:4 AMP

Sometimes we approach our prayer time with God with a list in hand, much like a child at Christmastime. Other times we approach the Lord with fear leading the way. "What happens if He doesn't respond like I hope?" Though we don't need to come with a Christmas list in hand, we do need to confidently approach our heavenly Father and make our requests with joy. He loves us, after all! So, draw near!

Continued Prayers

Continue in prayer, and watch in the same with thanksgiving.
COLOSSIANS 4:2 KJV

Are you the sort of person who gives up easily? Does your faith waver if God doesn't respond to your prayers right away? Don't give up, and don't stop praying, particularly if you're believing God for something that seems impossible. Be like that little widow woman in the Bible. . .the one who pestered the judge until he responded. Just keep at it. As you continue in prayer, keep a joyful heart, filled with expectation.

Enjoying Life

Let all who seek You
rejoice and be glad in You; and let
those who love Your salvation say
continually, "Let God be magnified."
. . .You are my help and my deliverer.

PSALM 70:4–5 NASB

Sometimes we approach God robotically: "Lord, please do this for me. Lord, please do that." We're convinced we'll be happy, if only God grants our wishes like a genie in a bottle. We're going about this backward! We should start by praising God. Thank Him for life, health, and the many answered prayers. Our joyous praise will remind us just how blessed we already are! Then—out of genuine relationship—we make our requests known.

Joy Leads the Way

Then will I go unto the altar of God,
unto God my exceeding joy:
yea, upon the harp will I praise thee,
O God my God.

PSALM 43:4 KJV

We're instructed to come into the Lord's
presence with a joy-filled heart. . .to praise
our way into the throne room. Perhaps
you're not a musician. You don't own an
instrument and only sing in the shower.
Don't let that keep you from approaching
the altar with a song of praise on your lips.
Today, let joy lead the way, and may your
praises be glorious!

Provision

Daily Provision

"Who provides food for the raven
when its young cry out to God and
wander about for lack of food?"

JOB 38:41 NIV

Does it fill your heart with joy to know that God provides for your needs? He makes provision. . .both in seasons of want and seasons of plenty. There's no need to strive. No need to worry. He's got it all under control. If He provides food for the ravens, then surely He knows how to give you everything you need when you need it. So, praise Him!

Joyous Provision

And my God will meet all your needs
according to his glorious riches
in Christ Jesus.

PHILIPPIANS 4:19 NIV

Sometimes God goes overboard when it's
time to make provision. He blesses us above
and beyond what we could ask or think.
He not only meets our needs. . .He throws
in a bit of excess, just to watch us smile. If
you're in a season of abundant provision,
remember to share the joy! Pass on a
portion of what He has given you. And praise
Him! What an awesome God we serve!

Who Provides?

Consider the lilies how they grow:
they toil not, they spin not.
LUKE 12:27 KJV

Sometimes we look at our job as our
provision. We say things like, "I work for
my money." While it's true that we work
hard (and are rewarded with a paycheck),
we can't forget that God is our Provider. If
He cares for the lilies of the field—flowers
that bloom for such a short season—then
how much more does He care for us, His
children? What joy. . .realizing God loves
us enough to provide for our needs.

Joyfully Satisfied

**"I will abundantly bless her provision;
I will satisfy her needy with bread."**

PSALM 132:15 NASB

The Lord has promised to meet all of our
needs, according to His riches in glory.
His heart is for His people, especially the
poor and downtrodden. Today, as you seek
God about your own needs, ask Him how
you can help meet the needs of the less
fortunate in your community. What a joy
it will be to reach out to others. . .even if
you're also in need.

Hearts Filled with Joy

"He provides you with plenty of food
and fills your hearts with joy."
ACTS 14:17 NIV

When we think about provision, we usually think in terms of money, don't we? Getting the bills paid. Having food in the pantry. Making sure our needs are met. But what about our emotional needs? Does the Lord make provision in that area, as well? Of course! According to this scripture, He fills our hearts with joy. What an awesome God we serve!

Salvation

Joy in Heaven

"In the same way, there is more joy
in heaven over one lost sinner who
repents and returns to God than over
ninety-nine others who are righteous
and haven't strayed away!"

LUKE 15:7 NLT

What a party heaven throws when one person comes to know the Lord! Can't you see it now? The angels let out a shout! The trumpeters play their victory chant. All of heaven reacts joyfully to the news. Oh, that we would respond with such joy to the news of a lost soul turning to the Lord. What a celebration!

Rejoicing in Salvation

Then my soul will rejoice in the LORD
and delight in his salvation.

PSALM 35:9 NIV

Do you remember what it felt like to put your trust in Christ for the first time? Likely, you've never experienced anything else that brought such joy, such release. Oh, the joy of that salvation experience. The overwhelming realization that the God of the universe loves you—enough to send His only Son to die on a cross so that you could have eternal life. There's no greater joy than the joy of salvation.

Restored Joy

Restore unto me the joy of thy
salvation; and uphold me
with thy free spirit.

PSALM 51:12 KJV

When you restore your home, you return it to its prior state—its best possible condition. But is it possible to restore joy? Can you really get it back once lost? Of course you can! Joy is a choice and can be restored with a single decision. Decide today. Make up your mind. Get ready for the renovation to take place as you ask the Lord to restore the joy of your salvation.

Wells of Salvation

With joy you will drink deeply from
the fountain of salvation!

ISAIAH 12:3 NLT

In biblical times, women would go to the
local well for water. They would drop the
bucket down, down, down, then lift it up,
filled to the brim. Today, the Lord wants
you to reach down into His well of salvation
and, with great joy, draw up the bucket.
Remember how He saved you? Delivered
you? Remember His grace? Is your bucket
filled to the brim? If so, then that's
something to celebrate!

The Rock of
Our Salvation

O come, let us sing
unto the LORD:
let us make a joyful noise to
the rock of our salvation.

PSALM 95:1 KJV

God never changes. He's the same—
yesterday, today, and forever. We go through
a multitude of changes in our lives, but,
praise God, He's consistent. Doesn't that
bring joy to your heart, to realize that the
Creator of the universe is our Rock? And
don't you feel like celebrating when you
realize that, no matter how much you mess
up, His promise of salvation is true? Praise
be to the Lord, our Rock!

Sorrow and Suffering

Joy in Place of Tears

They that sow in tears shall reap in joy.

PSALM 126:5 KJV

Periods of great sorrow are unavoidable. Perhaps the death of a loved one has left you floundering. Or maybe your heart has been broken by someone you thought you could trust. If you've been through an earth-shaking change—one you weren't expecting or feel you didn't deserve—then turn to the One who can replenish you. God will walk with you through this valley and promises to replace your tears with joy.

A Compassionate Heart

Break forth into joy, sing together,
you waste places of Jerusalem! For
the LORD has comforted His people,
He has redeemed Jerusalem.

ISAIAH 52:9 NKJV

Have you ever knelt to comfort a child
as the tears flowed down his or her little
cheeks? If so, then you understand the
heart of your Daddy God as He gently wipes
away your tears during times of sorrow.
He comforts as only a Father can, bringing
hope where there is no hope and joy where
there is no joy. What a compassionate God
we serve!

Sorrows. . .Be Gone!

"I tell you the truth, you will weep
and mourn while the world rejoices.
You will grieve, but your grief
will turn to joy."

JOHN 16:20 NIV

Imagine you're washing a load of white
towels. One of them is badly stained. You
add bleach to the wash load and let it run its
cycle. Afterward, you can't tell which towel is
which! The same is true when we allow God
to wash away our sorrows. When all is said
and done, all that remains is the joy!

Partakers of Joy

But rejoice that you participate
in the sufferings of Christ,
so that you may be overjoyed
when his glory is revealed.

1 PETER 4:13 NIV

Ever feel like you've signed on for the
suffering but not the joy? We are called to be
partakers in Christ's sufferings. We wouldn't
really know Him if we didn't walk in the
valleys occasionally. But, praise God! We are
also partakers in His glorious resurrection.
We have the power of the cross to spur us on!
The time has come to trade in those sorrows.
Reach for His unspeakable joy.

A Deeper Joy

You changed my sorrow into dancing.
You took away my clothes of sadness,
and clothed me in happiness.

PSALM 30:11 NCV

Sometimes despair can feel like a deep
well. You feel trapped. Can't seem to find
your way out to the daylight above. Oh,
friend! As deep as your well of sorrow might
be, there is a deeper joy. Finding it requires
resting your head against the Savior's chest,
listening for His heartbeat until it beats in
sync with yours. Today, dig deep. . .and find
that joy.

Temptation

Count It All Joy!

Consider it pure joy, my brothers, whenever you face trials of many kinds.

JAMES 1:2 NIV

Temptations abound. We face them at every turn. On the television. In our conversations with friends. On the Internet. Today, as you contemplate the many temptations that life has to offer, count it all joy! The enemy knows we belong to the King of kings. That's the only reason he places stumbling blocks in our way. Next time he rears his ugly head, use joy as a weapon to fight him off.

Deliver Us. . .with Joy!

And lead us not into temptation, but
deliver us from evil: For thine is the
kingdom, and the power, and
the glory, for ever. Amen.

MATTHEW 6:13 KJV

Have you ever been ensnared by the
enemy? Led into temptation? Caught in his
trap? When you give your heart to Christ,
you are set free from your past, delivered
from the bondage of sin. Talk about a
reason to celebrate. Nothing is more
glorious than being led out of a prison cell
into the sunlight. Oh, joyous freedom!
Today, praise God for the things He has
delivered you from.

The Spirit Is Willing

"Watch and pray, lest you enter into
temptation. The spirit indeed is
willing, but the flesh is weak."

MARK 14:38 NKJV

We've got to be on our guard for
unexpected attacks. Temptation can strike
at any point. We might feel strong—might
convince ourselves we're not vulnerable—
but our flesh is weak! We often end up
giving in, even when we're determined not
to. Today, ask the Lord to prepare you for
any temptations that might come your way.
Then, with joy in your heart, be on your
guard!

A Joyous Crown

Blessed is the man who perseveres under trial, because when he has stood the test, he will receive the crown of life that God has promised to those who love him.

JAMES 1:12 NIV

We are so focused on the joys of this life that we sometimes forget the exquisite joys yet to come in the next. Enduring and overcoming temptation can bring us great satisfaction here on earth, but imagine the crown of life we're one day going to receive. Nothing can compare! Oh, the joy of eternal life. Oh, the thrill of that joyous crown.

Rooted and Grounded

"Those on the rock are the ones who
receive the word with joy when they
hear it, but they have no root.
They believe for a while, but in
the time of testing they fall away."

LUKE 8:13 NIV

Imagine a sturdy oak tree, one that's been growing for decades. Its roots run deep. It's grounded. When the storms of life strike, that tree is going to stand strong. Now think of your own roots. Do they run deep? When temptations strike, will you stand strong? Dig into the Word. Receive it with joy. Let it be your foundation. Plant yourself and let your roots run deep.

Thankfulness

A Thankful Heart

Let the peace of Christ rule in
your hearts, since as members of
one body you were called to peace.
And be thankful.

COLOSSIANS 3:15 NIV

Have you ever received really great news. . .
unexpectedly? Remember the inexplicable
joy that rose up as you received it? You
didn't conjure it up; the joy came quite
naturally. Today, the news is good! God
loves you! He cares for your needs and
surrounds you on every side. He is your
defense. As you contemplate these things,
watch out! Joy is sure to fill your heart!

Hem Your Blessings

Everything God created is good,
and to be received with thanks.
1 TIMOTHY 4:4 MSG

Sometimes we walk through seasons of blessing and forget to be grateful. It's easy, with the busyness of life, to overlook the fact that Someone has made provision to cover the monthly bills. Someone has graced us with good health. Someone has given us friends and loved ones to share our joys and sorrows. Today, pause a moment and thank the Lord for the many gifts He's poured out. Hem in those blessings!

Thanks. . .Again!

How can we thank God enough
for you in return for all the joy
we have in the presence of
our God because of you?

1 THESSALONIANS 3:9 NIV

Think of the people God has placed in
your life—your family members, friends,
coworkers, and other loved ones. They
bring such joy and happiness to your life,
don't they? Now contemplate this. . .what if
you'd never met any of them? How different
would your life be? These folks are such a
gift! God has given them to you as a special
present. . .one you need to remember to
thank Him for.

Thanking Him. . .Publicly!

Give thanks unto the LORD,
call upon his name, make known
his deeds among the people.

1 CHRONICLES 16:8 KJV

It's one thing to thank God in the privacy of your prayer closet; it's another to openly talk about the amazing things He's done in your life in front of a watching world. The words of your mouth, lifted up in joyful testimony, could have an amazing impact on those around you. So, go ahead. . .thank Him publicly. Share the things He's done with people you come in contact with. Make His deeds known!

Thanks Be to God!

I am grateful that God always makes it possible for Christ to lead us to victory.

2 CORINTHIANS 2:14 CEV

God has created us to be victors, not victims. We are image-bearers of Christ and born to triumph! So, how do you see yourself today? Have you made up your mind to overcome in the areas where you've struggled? One way to assure your victory is to praise God for it. . .even before it happens. That's right! Praise your way through! Oh, the joy of triumphing in Christ!

Vision

A Royal Vision

Yes, joyful are those who live
like this! Joyful indeed are those
whose God is the LORD.

PSALM 144:15 NLT

How wonderful to realize you're God's child. He loves you and wants nothing but good for you. Doesn't knowing you're His daughter send waves of joy through your soul? How happy we are when we recognize that we are princesses. . .children of the most high God! Listen closely as He whispers royal secrets in your ear. Your heavenly Father offers you keys to the Kingdom. . .and vision for the road ahead.

"Happy Is He. . ." (or She!)

Where there is no vision,
the people perish: but he that keep-
eth the law, happy is he.

PROVERBS 29:18 KJV

Ever wish you could see into tomorrow?
Wish you knew what was coming around the
bend? While we can't see into the future, we
can prepare for it by trusting God to bring
us His very best. And while our "literal"
vision can't glimpse the unseen tomorrow,
we can prepare for it by staying close to the
Lord and spending time in His Word. Peace
and joy come when we trust God with our
future!

A Joyous Stand

May he give you the desire of
your heart and make all your plans
succeed. We will shout for joy when
you are victorious and will lift up our
banners in the name of our God.

PSALM 20:4–5 NIV

It's hard to have a vision for tomorrow if
you're not excited about today! Each day is a
gift, after all, and an opportunity to live for
Christ. Today, take a stand for the things you
believe in. Lift high His name. Not only will
you bring joy to His heart (and your own),
you will find yourself looking forward to a
joy-filled tomorrow.

An Ear to Hear

He that hath an ear,
let him hear what the Spirit
saith unto the churches.

REVELATION 2:17 KJV

We need to "lean in" to the Lord on a daily basis. Listen to His still, small voice. Catch a glimpse of His vision for the church. Ride on the wind of the Spirit. Today, as you draw close to the Lord, listen closely. What is He speaking into your life? May your joy be full as you "tune in" to the voice of the Holy Spirit.

Seeing the Invisible

Now faith is being sure of what we hope for and certain of what we do not see.

HEBREWS 11:1 NIV

You must look at your future as hopeful, and filled with wonderful "what ifs." No, you're not promised tomorrow. But if you give up on your hopes and dreams, if you lose sight of the plans the Lord has laid on your heart, they will surely not come to pass. Trust God to make the invisible. . .visible. And in the meantime, rejoice! You have a lot to look forward to!

Wisdom

Wisdom. . .What Joy!

Happy is the man who finds wisdom,
and the man who gains
understanding.

PROVERBS 3:13 NKJV

Imagine you've lost a priceless jewel—one passed down from your grandmother to your mother and then to you. You search everywhere, under every rock, in every closet. Still, you can't find it. Finally, in the least likely spot. . .you discover it! Joy floods your soul! Now imagine that "jewel" is wisdom. You've stumbled across it, and oh, what a treasure! Talk about a happy find!

The Key to Happiness

He who heeds the word wisely
will find good, and whoever
trusts in the Lord, happy is he.

PROVERBS 16:20 NKJV

Want the key to true happiness? Try wisdom. When others around you are losing their heads, losing their cool, and losing sleep over their decisions, choose to react differently. Step up to the plate. Handle matters wisely. Wise choices always lead to joyous outcomes. And along the way, you will be setting an example for others around you to follow. So, c'mon. . .get happy! Get wisdom!

Walking Uprightly

Folly is joy to him who is destitute
of discernment, but a man of
understanding walks uprightly.

PROVERBS 15:21 NKJV

Ever noticed that people who have
something to hide don't look others in
the eye? Their gaze shifts up, down, and
all around. But those who walk uprightly
can look others in the eye without guilt or
shame. Live wisely. Hold your head high.
Look folks in the eye. Let wisdom lead the
way and watch as joy follows!

Seek Out Wisdom

I applied mine heart to know, and
to search, and to seek out wisdom.

ECCLESIASTES 7:25 KJV

Remember when you participated in your
first Easter egg hunt? You searched under
every bush, every tree until you found one
of those shiny eggs. The quest for wisdom
is much like that. You've got to look under a
lot of shrubs to find it, especially in this day
and age. Oh, but what a prize! Today, as you
apply your heart to the Word of God, seek
out wisdom. What a joyous treasure!

The Words of
My Mouth

**She speaks with wisdom, and faithful
instruction is on her tongue.**

PROVERBS 31:26 NIV

Have you ever known someone who
epitomized wisdom? What set her apart
from others of your acquaintance? A
truly wise person thinks carefully before
speaking and only opens her mouth when
wisdom is ready to flow out. Kindness is on
her tongue. There's great joy in "becoming"
wise in this way. Today, guard your tongue!
Think before you speak. By doing so, you
bring joy to others. . .and yourself.

Witness

A Net of Love

No one has ever seen God; but if we love one another, God lives in us and his love is made complete in us.

1 JOHN 4:12 NIV

It's hard to be a good witness if you've got a sour expression on your face. People aren't usually won to the Lord by grumpy friends and coworkers. If you hope to persuade people that life in Jesus is the ultimate, then you've got to let your enthusiasm shine through. Before you reach for the net, spend some time on your knees, asking for an infusion of joy. Then, go catch some fish!

A Witness to the Nations

"Go therefore and make disciples
of all the nations."

MATTHEW 28:19 NASB

Have you ever pondered the mandate in
Matthew's Gospel to go into all the world
and preach the gospel? Ever feel like you're
not doing your part? God calls us to be
witnesses where we are—to bloom where
we're planted. Imagine the joy of leading
a neighbor or a friend to the Lord. So,
instead of fretting over not doing enough,
delight in the fact that you are usable. . .
right where you are.

Powerful Witnesses

"But you will receive power
when the Holy Spirit
has come upon you;
and you shall be My witnesses
both in Jerusalem, and in all Judea
and Samaria, and even to the
remotest part of the earth."

ACTS 1:8 NASB

Want to experience real joy in your life? Then become a powerful witness. The most effective witness for Christ is one who is wholly surrendered to God's will, and who has invited the Holy Spirit to do a transforming work in her life. After all, we can't really share the good news if our lives haven't been truly changed. Allow the Lord to renovate you from the inside out—then change your world!

Blooming for
All to See

Since God chose you to be the holy
people he loves, you must clothe
yourselves with tenderhearted
mercy, kindness, humility,
gentleness, and patience.

COLOSSIANS 3:12 NLT

Have you ever noticed that we're naturally
drawn to people who are fun to be around. . .
people who radiate joy? They are like a
garden of thornless roses: They put off a
beautiful aroma and draw people quite
naturally. If you want to win people to the
Lord, then woo them with your kindness.
Put off an inviting aroma. Win them with
your love. Radiate joy!

Bearing Witness

The life appeared; we have seen it and
testify to it, and we proclaim to you
the eternal life, which was with the
Father and has appeared to us.

1 JOHN 1:2 NIV

We don't have to work hard at being good
witnesses when we're walking in close
relationship with the Lord. Our witness will
flow quite naturally out of our relationship
with God. In other words, we "are" witnesses,
simply by living the life He's called us to live.
And by living the life, we point others toward
eternal life. Now, that will cause joy to rise up
in your soul!

Work

Not Withholding

Anything I wanted, I would take.
I denied myself no pleasure. I even
found great pleasure in hard work,
a reward for all my labors.

ECCLESIASTES 2:10 NLT

Work beckons. Deadlines loom. You're
trying to balance your home life against your
work life, and it's overwhelming. Take heart!
It is possible to rejoice in your labors—to
find pleasure in the day-to-day tasks.
At work or at play. . .let the Lord cause a
song of joy to rise up in your heart.

Joy in Your Work

Go, eat your food with gladness,
and drink your wine with
a joyful heart, for it is now
that God favors what you do.

ECCLESIASTES 9:7 NIV

Ever feel like nothing you do is good
enough? Your boss is frustrated over
something you've done wrong. The kids
are complaining. Your neighbors are even
upset at you. How wonderful to read that
God accepts our works, even when we feel
lacking. He encourages us to go our way with
a merry heart, completely confident that we
are accepted in the Beloved.

Joyous
Petitions

Delight yourself in the LORD
and he will give you the
desires of your heart.

PSALM 37:4 NIV

What are the deepest desires of your
heart? Ponder that question a moment.
If you could really do—or have—what you
longed for, what would that be? The key to
receiving from the Lord is delighting in
Him. Draw near. Spend time with your head
against His shoulder, feeling His heartbeat.
Ask that your requests come into alignment
with His will. Then, with utmost joy, make
your petitions known.

The Fork in the Road

What does a man get for all the toil
and anxious striving with which
he labors under the sun?

ECCLESIASTES 2:22 NIV

Imagine you're approaching a fork in the
road. You're unsure of which way to turn.
If you knew ahead of time that the road to
the right would be filled with joy and the
road to left would lead to sorrow, wouldn't
it make the decision easier? Today, as you
face multiple decisions, ask God to lead you
down the right road.

The Fruit of Your Labor

You will eat the fruit of your labor;
blessings and prosperity will be yours.

PSALM 128:2 NIV

We're always waiting for the payoff, aren't we? When we've put a lot of effort into a project, for example, we hope to see good results. The Word of God promises that we will eat the fruit of our labor—that we will eventually experience blessings and prosperity. So, all of that hard work will be worth it. But remember, the joy is in the journey! It's not just in the payoff.

Scripture Index

Job

Psalms